THE GREATEST SHOWMAN

ORIGINAL SONGS BY

BENJ PASEK & JUSTIN PAUL

Special thanks to Alex Lacamoire

ISBN 978-1-5400-0711-7

7777 W. BLUEMOUND RD. P.O. BOX 13819 MILWAUKEE, WI 53213

In Australia Contact:
Hal Leonard Australia Pty. Ltd.
4 Lentara Court
Cheltenham, Victoria, 3192 Australia
Email: ausadmin@halleonard.com.au

Visit Hal Leonard Online at
www.halleonard.com

THE GREATEST SHOW

Words and Music by BENJ PASEK,
JUSTIN PAUL and RYAN LEWIS

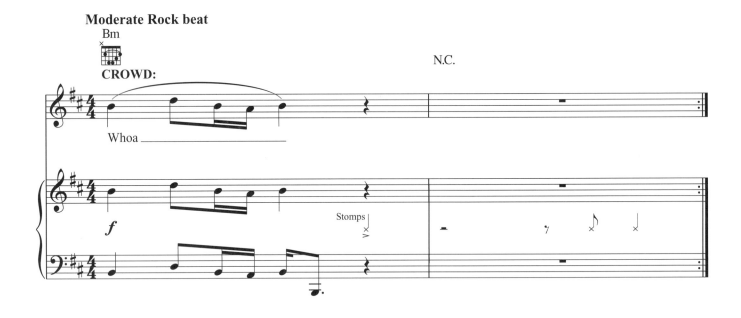

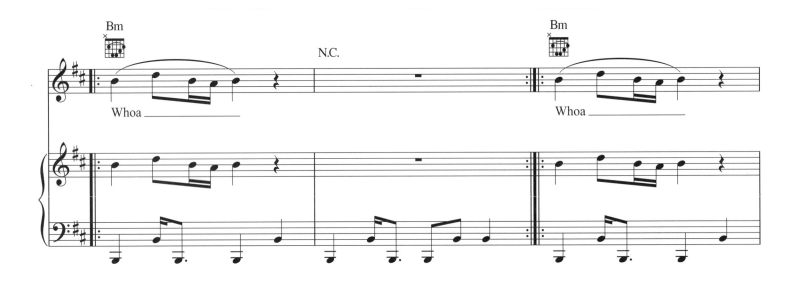

COME ALIVE

Words and Music by BENJ PASEK
and JUSTIN PAUL

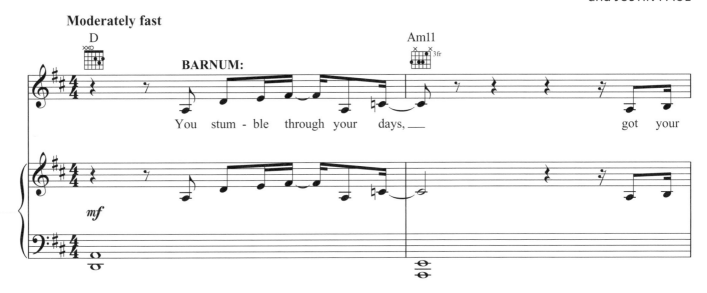

BARNUM: You stum-ble through your days, ___ got your

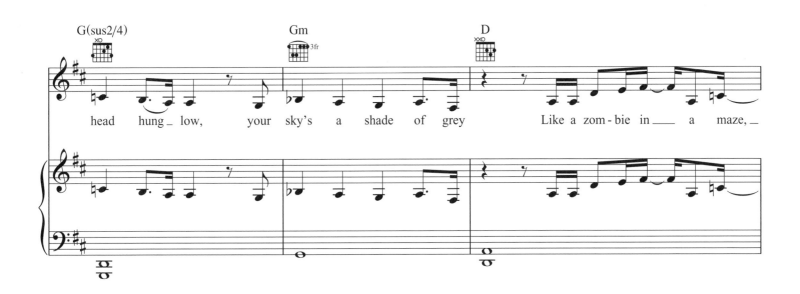

head hung _ low, your sky's a shade of grey Like a zom-bie in __ a maze, __

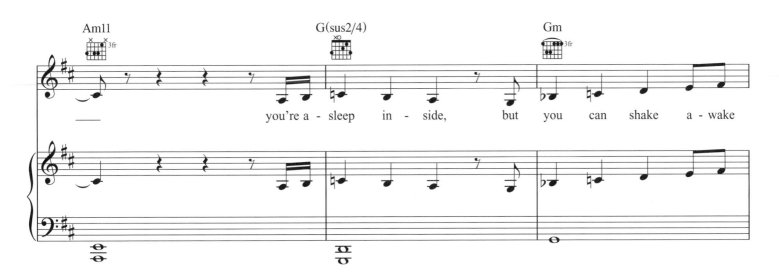

__ you're a-sleep in - side, but you can shake a-wake

- in' with your eyes __ wide o - pen

And we know __ we can't go back a-gain to the world __ that we were liv-in' in, 'cause we're dream -

- in' with our eyes __ wide o-pen

So come a-live! ____

metal shaker

Vamp

BARNUM/ODDITIES:

Come one, __ come all, ____ come in, ____ come on ____

low drums

A MILLION DREAMS

Words and Music by BENJ PASEK
and JUSTIN PAUL

*Barnum vocal line written an octave higher throughout.

THE OTHER SIDE

Words and Music by BENJ PASEK
and JUSTIN PAUL

NEVER ENOUGH

Words and Music by BENJ PASEK
and JUSTIN PAUL

THIS IS ME

Words and Music by BENJ PASEK
and JUSTIN PAUL

TIGHTROPE

Words and Music by BENJ PASEK
and JUSTIN PAUL

*Lead vocal written an octave higher.

REWRITE THE STARS

Words and Music by BENJ PASEK
and JUSTIN PAUL

Moderately fast

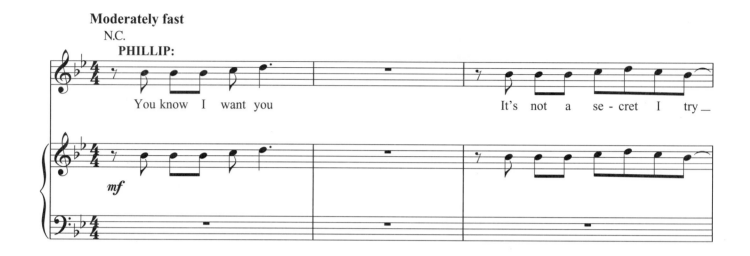

You know I want you   It's not a se-cret I try__

__ to hide __   I know you want me,

so don't keep say-in' our hands __ are tied __   You claim it's not in the cards __

*Play cue note left hand on D.S.

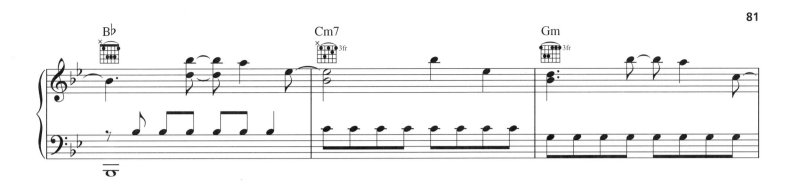

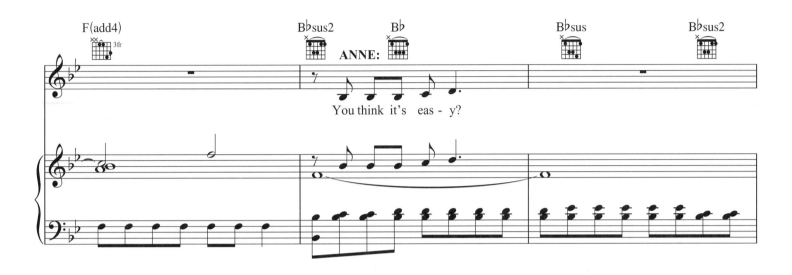

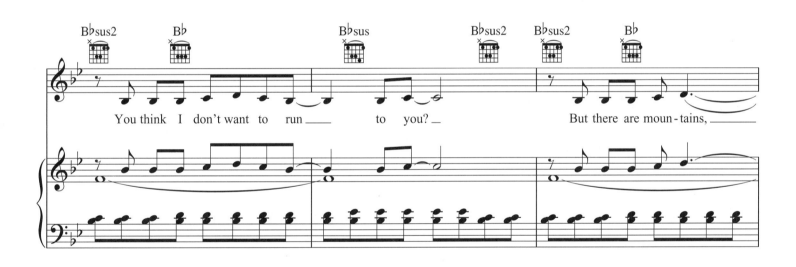

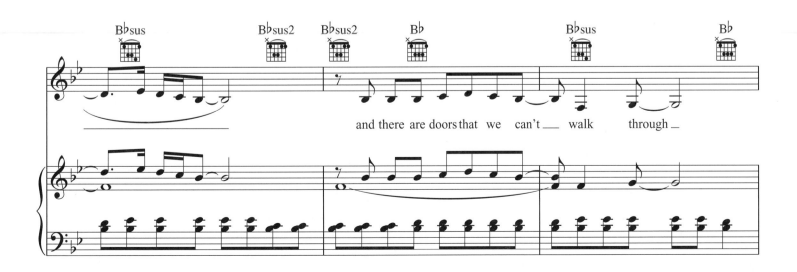

FROM NOW ON

Words and Music by BENJ PASEK
and JUSTIN PAUL

*1st verse: Lead vocal written two octaves higher.

on what's wait-ed 'til to-mor-row starts to-night, to-

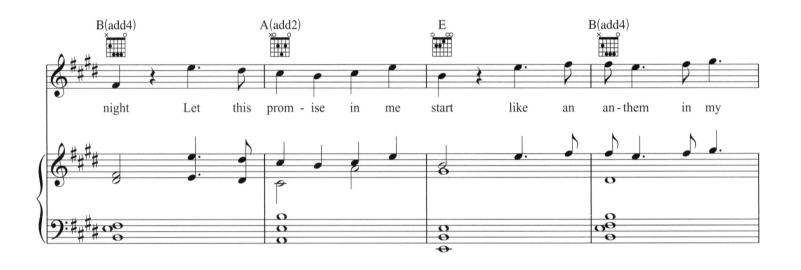

night Let this prom-ise in me start like an an-them in my

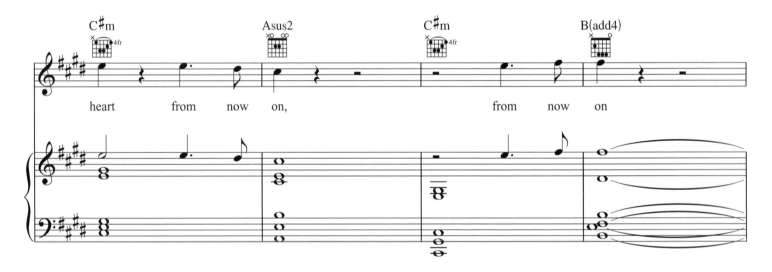

heart from now on, from now on

Moderately in 2

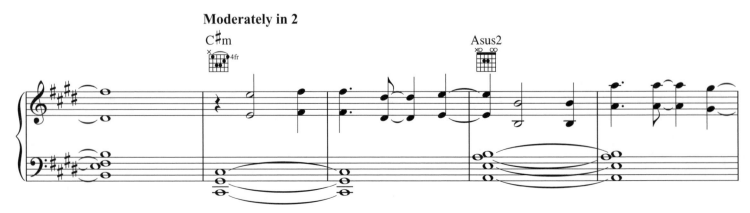

*Lead vocal written an octave higher.

ODDITIES:

And we will come back home, and we will come back home,
(on)

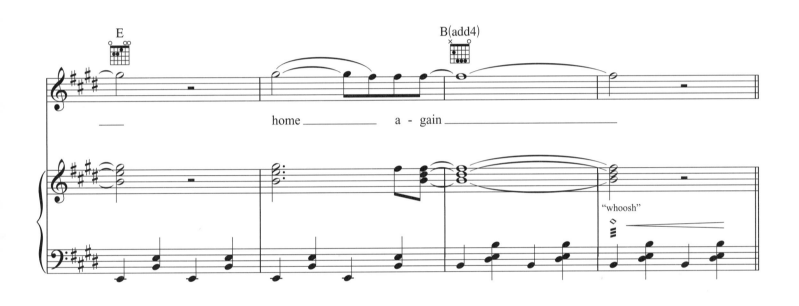

home a - gain

"whoosh"

BARNUM/ODDITIES:

From now on, from now

And we will come back home, and we will come back home,

Drums

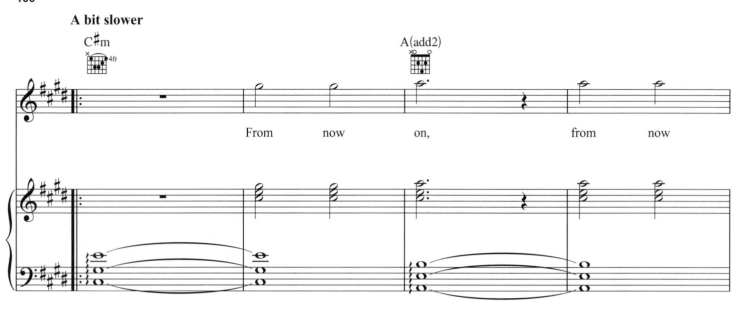

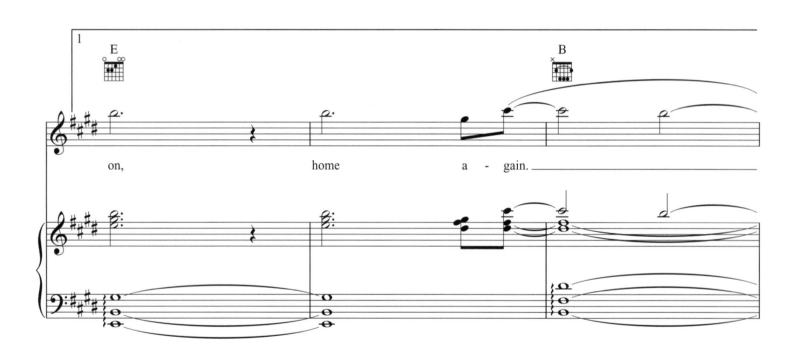

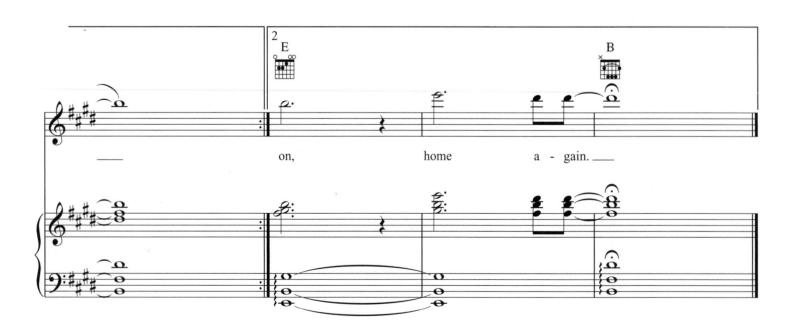